WITHOUT BEGINNING OR END

THE HUGH MacLENNAN POETRY SERIES

Editors: Allan Hepburn and Carolyn Smart

Recent titles in the series

whereabouts Edward Carson
The Tantramar Re-Vision Kevin Irie
Earth Words: Conversing with Three Sages John Reibetanz
Vlarf Jason Camlot
Unbecoming Neil Surkan
Bitter in the Belly John Emil Vincent
unfinishing Brian Henderson
Nuclear Family Jean Van Loon
Full Moon of Afraid and Craving Melanie Power
Rags of Night in Our Mouths Margo Wheaton
watching for life David Zieroth
Orchid Heart Elegies Zoë Landale
The House You Were Born In Tanya Standish McIntyre
The Decline and Fall of the Chatty Empire John Emil Vincent
New Songs for Orpheus John Reibetanz
the swailing Patrick James Errington
movingparts Edward Carson
Murmuration: Marianne's Book John Baglow
Take the Compass Maureen Hynes
act normal nancy viva davis halifax
[about]ness Eimear Laffan
twofold Edward Carson
Whiny Baby Julie Paul
Metromorphoses John Reibetanz
Bridestones Miranda Pearson
Dreamcraft Peter Dale Scott
Water Quality Cynthia Woodman Kerkham
Without Beginning or End Jacqueline Bourque

Without Beginning or End

JACQUELINE BOURQUE

McGill-Queen's University Press

Montreal & Kingston • London • Chicago

ISBN 978-0-2280-2261-9 (paper)
ISBN 978-0-2280-2262-6 (ePDF)
ISBN 978-0-2280-2263-3 (ePUB)

Legal deposit third quarter 2024
Bibliothèque nationale du Québec

Printed in Canada on acid-free paper that is 100% ancient forest free
(100% post-consumer recycled), processed chlorine free

Funded by the Government of Canada   Financé par le gouvernement du Canada   Canada Council for the Arts   Conseil des arts du Canada

We acknowledge the support of the Canada Council for the Arts.

Nous remercions le Conseil des arts du Canada de son soutien.

McGill-Queen's University Press in Montreal is on land which long served
as a site of meeting and exchange amongst Indigenous Peoples, including
the Haudenosaunee and Anishinabeg nations. In Kingston it is situated
on the territory of the Haudenosaunee and Anishinaabek. We acknowledge
and thank the diverse Indigenous Peoples whose footsteps have marked
these territories on which peoples of the world now gather.

Library and Archives Canada Cataloguing in Publication

Title: Without beginning or end / Jacqueline Bourque.

Names: Bourque, Jacqueline, author.

Series: Hugh MacLennan poetry series.

Description: Series statement: The Hugh MacLennan poetry series

Identifiers: Canadiana (print) 20240396456 | Canadiana (ebook)
20240396464 | ISBN 9780228022619 (softcover) |
ISBN 9780228022626 (PDF) | ISBN 9780228022633 (ePUB)

Subjects: LCGFT: Poetry.

Classification: LCC PS8603.O95563 W58 2024 | DDC C811/.6—dc23

This book was designed and typeset by Marquis Interscript
in 9.5/13 Sabon.
Copyediting by Lisa Aitken.

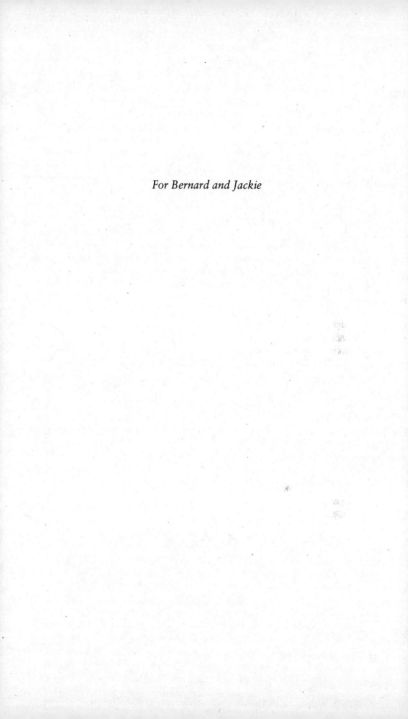

For Bernard and Jackie

We move
forward to bend and catch our past ...

Catherine Graham
Her Red Hair Rises with the Wings of Insects

CONTENTS

FALLING FROM HIGH TREES

I Dropped from the Sky That Morning   3
My Father's Topcoat   5
Cap-Pelé Coastline at 4:30 a.m.   6
Infusion   7
At Dawn, I Open   8
A Letter Slips into the Coastline   9
Preparations   10
Ancestral Waters   11

AERIAL VAGABONDS

Between Thoughts   15
On a Swath of Land Bordered by
the Northumberland Strait   16
Vatican II Opens the Church's Window   17
Two Continents   18
There Is No Why   19
Philippe Petit as Prometheus   20
Posthumous Visit   21
Divine Motion, 1992   22
Why Père Chabert Wept When He Read
Baudelaire to His First-Year University Class   23
Père Chabert and the Passion   24
A House in Chile, a School in L'Acadie   25
In the Background   26
Père Chabert's Legacy   27
You Will Walk along the River   28

Contents

ON CANVAS

Enigma of the Arrival and the Afternoon   31
The Dream of Constantine   32
Metaphysical Composition   34
Theseus and the Minotaur   35
*Dream Caused by the Flight of a Bee
around a Pomegranate a Second Before Awakening*   36
Detail of the Saint Anthony Panel from
the *Hermit Saints Triptych*, ca. 1505   37
*Icon of the Allegorical Ladder
of Saint John Climacus*   38
Allegory of Immortality   39
Drop Curtain for the Ballet *Parade*   41
The City Rises   42
Time Is a River without Banks   43
The Tower of Babel   44
Magdalene with Two Flames   45

WITHOUT BEGINNING OR END

John   49
Marie   50
Rain in Cap-Pelé   51
Topcoat   52
Train to Boston   53
Shining Knight   54
Christmas Eve   55
John William Becomes a Breadwinner at Fourteen   56
The Joan Hat   57
And for a Father Hear a Child   58
The Pod's Dark Seeds   59
Goddess of Nightfall   60

Contents

The Children Now Scattered   61
My Grandmother Marie   62
My Grandfather John   63

Notes   65
Acknowledgments   67

FALLING FROM HIGH TREES

I DROPPED FROM THE SKY
THAT MORNING

I.

Untethered. A clump of bananas.

It didn't occur to me that I was no longer attached
to the ligatures of life, that I had fallen from high trees.

Below, I knew something had shifted. It was rather
a limpness, a disconnection with life. The days that
followed, I kept detaching, as if tumbling. A dramatic
shift in my positioning,

I noticed how grounded Bernard and Jackie remained.
My own connections were non-existent – medical
professionals came but nothing of heft resulted.
I remained on the floor, ready to let go completely.

2.

I venture out on the moor, search for movement on water.

Owing to medication, or sheer will, I reconnect to source.

Much is unknown.

This is the land where I reside.

I walk along fabric edge until it reveals itself, shows
    me the way, or that there is no longer a way.

MY FATHER'S TOPCOAT

I awaken to the vanishing night.

Winter, like a housecoat, outlines trees, lumbers through
the quiet and solemn house.

At the core of everything: love.

The scene at the train station where my father worked
as a youth. He carries his topcoat. The fabric stiff and
new. A cigarette held between two fingers.

Late in life, I was gifted with purpose. It's my journey to
struggle towards, to hang on (as if to the tail of a racing
horse); until my clutch is firm and determined.

I pick up towels and furniture strewn over this now
strange land. The creatures that survive swell or release
water, depending on the tide's course.

Prince Edward Island shields the Northumberland Strait
and keeps it gentle, though the strait throws tantrums –
like the one just witnessed.

At this hour, day has begun to infiltrate the shore's
seamless darkness with exact brightness.

My nature is changing. My penumbra, with its perfect light
and impeccable shadows mimics the process of leaving,
bringing with it an assured knowing, a wolverine tongue.

Dawn is a barroom, the morning after,
Macbeth flung on the floor

    where someone said look up
           and there,
blindingly,

    a sophomore soared,
    seizing the inconclusive.

Valves watertight.

    The way he held his breath –
    a buoy, filling with light.

the cottage door to the scent of marram grass.

I walk the solitary coastline, spotting a blue heron as he
wades. He seems to be in a sacred place, inside a dome
of silence.

A cormorant, further along, is its antithesis. Its tar-like
plumage is not waterproof and turns into a shock of
disgruntled angles. I'm reminded of a large black umbrella
that a gust of wind has turned inside out – yanked off its
metal frame.

The heron calms me.

The cormorant unsettles.

In my palliative months,
the cormorant leaves me
at peace, disintegrating
with the exhalation of a Buddha.

A LETTER SLIPS INTO THE COASTLINE

The Northumberland disappears into Prince Edward
Island's sand dunes. I remain on the opposite shore:
its features at night are borderless and imposing.

Since the doctors gave me a stage four diagnosis,
I've experienced moments of intense anxiety.

The people who have left before me did not send post
to advise on the transition.

I'm alone, slipping my own letter into the coastline.

PREPARATIONS

My shadow precedes me as it glides against landscape.

I am transforming.

My grandfather's gabled-roof house stands along the cliffs that trace the coastline.

The adults are in the kitchen preparing the summer dinner. My mother heads for the patch of chives growing on the right side of the porch ledge. She carries a pair of kitchen shears and a white tea cloth.

Kneeling beside the onions, she snips. Returns to the kitchen hubbub where she throws the chopped chives in the cast iron skillet and sautés them in butter with the leftover cubed potatoes we had at lunch.

I have developed a taste for this delicacy. The ritual.

I am alone in shallow water under an early morning sun. The pool is conical, the kind of place I could rest.

I received an edict. That is how things are done.

Later, my family and friends will gather. Some will engage; others will keep to themselves.

As the day draws to an end, people will return home with those they have chosen. Some will remain unmoved.

AERIAL VAGABONDS

The city lifts its brow from daybreak's fog
as a lover emerges from a steaming shower.
Talc powders the maples with silence – prologue
to morning, dash between thoughts.
Taut as the cable Philippe Petit walks:
Il joue avec le vent, cause avec le nuage,
foot lifts, slides close, hugs wire.
What is it that tugs inside? Why hyphenate
polarities? Charlie Parker rests on the brink
of breath, a pause that becomes his creative
shibboleth. Surf's musical beatitude
spellbinds Pablo Neruda at his desk.

ON A SWATH OF LAND BORDERED
BY THE NORTHUMBERLAND STRAIT

Baudelaire sends poems, anonymously, to Mme Sabatier –
L'élixir de ta bouche où l'amour se pavane.
Across the Atlantic, Acadian nuns and priests profess
vows to a loving God, their black robes swishing
through the Acadian day. The orders plant colleges
(all-girl, all-boy) like saplings, seed the land –
French Catholic students follow a strict classical
syllabus *amō, amās, amat, amāmus, amātis, amant.*
A century later, pavilions sprout on a hill edged
Petitcodiac's rivulet. The new French campus
sweeps Latin off the curriculum. Philippe Petit prances
back and forth between Notre Dame's twin towers.
Père Chabert struts into his co-ed classroom –
Baudelaire's love poems in his black leather briefcase.

VATICAN II OPENS
THE CHURCH'S WINDOW

The excavator plunges its arm into the hill
that rises like an afterthought at Moncton's edge.
The digging bucket crushes the small peace
that dozed underground, kills cardinal flowers,
musical bars, keys that signal sharps or flats.
Rain falls without mercy, as if wanting to remove.
Oblitero. Blot out. Obsolete papal imperatives
weigh knapsacks down as students teeter on boards
laid out for them over the new campus's mud. How
do they ignore this heft in their new balancing act –
flower power, free love, Jimi Hendrix, pot?
One false step, *je sens mon aile qui se casse*.
Philippe Petit opens a magazine to a photo
of the Twin Towers. He tears it out, pins it to his wall.

Campus life in a small New Brunswick town
the snow   solicitous   nestles into winter's curve –
        a lethargic flank of emblazoned ice crystals.
In an amphitheatre, one hundred cooped-up
first-year students yawn as Professor Chabert,
eyes squinting, right hand curled into a fist
        oblivious to his audience's opaque gaze
pounds the air to the rhythm of *Les Fleurs du Mal*.
Baudelaire's lines fall like birds crashing into windows –
Ma jeunesse ne fut qu'un ténébreux orage.
Philippe Petit, in a small town on another continent,
scrutinizes the tightrope's secrets,
gravity's mystery, the force that tightens his walk
from the known into the unknown.

This morning, amidst the flight of eagles
Petit perches on the tower's edge,
begins his high-wire poem: a single step
then another, so natural, the simplicity
of a smile, a line to the ringing
rushes of laughter inside as he dances
on the sky's ceiling. The wire arrows
into infinity. *Car il ne sera fait*
que de pure lumière. Joy rains like confetti
on the gathering crowds below
necks craned like fledglings,
a famished fluster of mouths – wide open.

Hoisted sky, cloud-capp'd twin columns,
one-inch-diameter cable, such is Petit's stage:
below, Lower Manhattan swarms with kinetic specks.
After eight passes, at the pinnacle of his pageantry,
he lies down on the wire   one leg dangles
into space. His skin becomes illusory
limitless, before a large-winged bird
lunges. Philippe remembers Prometheus
splayed on a crag, as an eagle devoured
the defier's liver. This aerial vagabondage
might irritate the gods of wind, wire and tower ...
Le Poète serein lève ses bras pieux.
He gathers gilded wingtips and walks
to the end of his rope, into the arms of the NYPD.

Three gold brushstrokes flicker through the haze
from rooftop flues, a façade surfacing
like a distant relative on your doorstep,
or a memory, uninvited – Professor Chabert
sports tortoiseshell glasses, a Beethoven-style
white mane, and holds *Les Fleurs du Mal*
like a hymnal. I recall his raspy voice –
Les morts, les pauvres morts, ont de grandes
douleurs – how fellow students dug elbows
into each other, laughed when he read
Baudelaire. Père Chabert articulated,
as if his life depended on each sound,
inserted deliberate breaths between words.
Then his face would shatter in a wash of tears.

In the vault above the nave, midair,
Philippe Petit, arrayed in a Chagall-inspired
ballet costume, blazes on the wire
Comme montent au ciel les soleils rajeunis.
Below, parishioners look up, their angled stare
like flying buttresses supporting his theatre.
     Religion, *religare*, to link people.
Cathedral silence grips every chest,
for fear that the slightest sibilance
could usher a dissonant doubt
into Petit's faith – that he will reach the other side,
alive. As the pipe organ ascends scales
he slide-steps rhythmically, an aging outlaw –
whose gruelling métier grants no mercy.

WHY PÈRE CHABERT WEPT
WHEN HE READ BAUDELAIRE TO HIS
FIRST-YEAR UNIVERSITY CLASS

Père Chabert sacrificed his beloved
when he committed to his vows – a promise
to hold heaven and hell in balance,
which demands the stamina of Ben Hur
tethering four Andalusians abreast. A promise
to remain celibate. Exhaustion and solitude usher
him toward the pain and bliss of the word ...
the Word was with God, and the Word
was God. At times, a line of poetry,
like a finger vibrato, revives a musical
tonality from his past. His priestly composure
loosens, allows tears as he recalls dancing
with her, long after the music had stopped.
J'eusse aimé voir son corps fleurir avec son âme.

Does his flock notice his leer lap the woman
in stilettos, his quivering urge
for cigarettes, his sympathy for Scotch?
No one speaks truth to him.
No one sees him brush his teeth,
wash his hands. The same hands
he washes during mass. Where do his vows
end? Where does he begin? Pontius Pilate
cleansed his hands as he surrendered
Jesus of Nazareth to the wolfish crowd.
Père Chabert knows that mob's mad hunger,
that wide maw inside which, left
unguarded, preys on blood. *Homme,
nul n'a sondé le fonds de tes abîmes.*

A HOUSE IN CHILE,
A SCHOOL IN L'ACADIE

Pablo Neruda's house stands on an outcrop
of bare black rocks. Resembling a ship,
with low ceilings and narrow passageways,
its maps, shells, figureheads,
and boats in bottles remind me of the sea
relics found in cottages on the edge
of the Northumberland Strait. Neruda's writing
space faces the Pacific's endlessness.
On his desk – a framed photo
of Charles Baudelaire. My youth
montant comme la mer sur le roc noir et nu
crashes over me with the sound
of my professor's voice reading from *Les Fleurs
du Mal* – unwittingly, unremittingly, unbowed.

Pablo Neruda gazes through daybreak mist.
Le chant du coq déchirant l'air brumeux startles.
He writes *For me you are a treasure more laden
with immensity than the sea.* Is that Charlie Parker
in the background, explaining the feeling
with alto sax notes, glass marbles gliding on velvet?
When my aunt Louisa made her religious vows,
she donned the name Soeur Marie Jean de la Croix,
a mantle whose meaning we wore down with usage,
unaware that John of the Cross was a Spanish mystic
poet – *my forehead on the lover I reclined.* His imagery
takes us beyond words, to something otherworldly.
John of the Cross and Charles Baudelaire watch on
as images stream from Pablo's pen, then take wing.

His theology was poetry, with its own rhyme
and its own reason, his life raft a Sorbonne PhD
in *Lettres Françaises*. The line he cast was wide
and it hooked a small world within me.
His bait was the word, a word which unattended
became longing, which unattended cracked
cement, which unattended woke me at dawn
with a deafening heartbeat, a pounding
that leapt outside and became a drum
that set the pace to my wandering, following
riverbanks, *Tel le vieux vagabond, piétinant
dans la boue*. It walked me until my breath
became wind, my mind became song
and my walking evolved into becoming.

and follow its coursing tide, downstream,
feel its embankment underfoot, the roundness
of its worn stones. Under skies feathered
with cloud, you will become the river's
nocturnal shadow, listen to sparrows and crows,
walk until you reach a wide mouth
that freely connects with open ocean.
Homme libre, toujours tu chériras la mer!
Tidal inlet of the sea, brackish place of water –
slightly salty – place where you began. Wade
into the estuary's bar-built flows
along its quarter moon shoreline.
Sit still in this nursery ground for spawning
and give the beach a name. Its name is your first poem.

ON CANVAS

ENIGMA OF THE ARRIVAL
AND THE AFTERNOON

by Giorgio de Chirico

This port proffers delayed
departures, imposed arrivals,
undecipherable advisories,
options that drain colour
from leaves. Scissor-clean
lines define its boundaries.

Above, yellow-green fades
into brown. Over an anvil
angle, a sliver of a ship's sail
caves with unfulfilled promises.
Its flag flies opposite wind.
Beyond tall harbour walls,
a rotunda boasts sun-drenched
epiphanies.

Two mummified figures stand
motionless at the edge of a chessboard
pavement. Discarded pawns.
Chiaroscuro divides the board.

Here, travellers bear no suitcases,
remain shadowless in the afternoon sun.

THE DREAM OF CONSTANTINE

by Piero della Francesca

The morning after his victory
Constantine walks the shoreline.

                He stops,
picks up a glinting piece
of aqua sea glass and remembers
his dream.

It arrived on battle day – an angel
holding a crucifix, its beam
sweeping over his tent, glowing
through a soldier's iron helmet
as if it were rice paper.

The cross carried the message
           by this sign you will conquer.

Constantine listened.
He rode into battle bearing the cross.
Won.

Francesca paints this scene
on the Basilica of Arezzo's wet wall
plaster. As the fresco dries, the vision
becomes one with the masonry

       not unlike Christianity
under Constantine's rule, inserting itself
into Rome's structure,
then Europe, and the world.

METAPHYSICAL COMPOSITION

by Giorgio de Chirico

On the canvas, a foot rises upwards
as if flying away,
                              the other foot
resigned

            on a ledge.

A large X engraved on a headstone
foreshadows the X-ray fluorescence
used to detangle de Chirico's
authentic works from his self-forgeries –
            he called them *verifalsi*,
true-fakes.

                        I strain to find my footing
this odd symmetry of objects brings up
            the Kh-22 missiles dropped
                              on a shopping mall
        a past I can't change
while the artist continues
                              to withhold
in tight clean lines.

THESEUS AND THE MINOTAUR

Master of the Cassoni Campana

Theseus's ship recedes into a scarab.
Ariadne's braids loosen in the wind.

She blames the Labyrinth –
his journey through it brought change.
She remembers how the feathers
on his helmet curled
like a preening swan's neck.
She remembers how he leaned
into her waxing crescent.

Theseus's youth was spent in the Labyrinth's
stygian corridors. At night, its chortles
abrade his ears.

He abandons Ariadne on the beach
as she sleeps, forgets to replace
the black sails on his ship with victory whites.

Centre stage, he flashes the stars
of his own constellation, kills
anyone who challenges his supremacy.

DREAM CAUSED BY THE FLIGHT
OF A BEE AROUND A POMEGRANATE
A SECOND BEFORE AWAKENING

by Salvador Dalí

"The difference between the Surrealists and me is that
I am a Surrealist."

Salvador Dalí

Gala floats above
    a slab of rock,
      her body like a wide yawn.
She shushes the bee,
reins in two pouncing tigers.

Before he met her, fits of laughter
barraged Dalí's words –
    his drift into hysteria
    a cube of sugar
    melting in tea.

Gala separates dream from reality:
muse, agent, shield, wife, mother.

Being a ward has its price:
without her, Dalí fails
to paint, to live. (After her death,
a freak fire in his bed burns
his arms and legs, Gala not there
to guard him from his flaming giraffes.)

DETAIL OF THE SAINT ANTHONY PANEL
FROM THE *HERMIT SAINTS TRIPTYCH*,
CA. 1505

by Hieronymus Bosch

Saint Anthony balances with a stake
as he plunges a vessel into water.
A nude woman wades in. He freezes.
Temptation everywhere.

This vision belongs to Bosch
placed beside a bird-like imp clenching
prey in its long beak,
tail fanned like a pearl-tipped Flamenco
haircomb.

Salvador Dalí, declaring he is not mad,
conjures the same temptation and renders
spider-legged elephants.

As if Bosch's garish characters
travelled through five centuries
of dreamscapes
and awoke in new paint, new brush.

A beautiful fever, flourishing.

ICON OF THE ALLEGORICAL LADDER
OF SAINT JOHN CLIMACUS

artist unknown

Lower Canvas

Demons pock, like bugs crushed
        on a windshield.
There a hellion harpoons the crook
        of a monk's neck
(dupe of mad pride), and another,
        hatchet in hand,
rides a cleric who arrows into hell
        (anger and avarice).

Upper Canvas

Holy men appear wooden on a ladder,
        quarter-moon mouths
downturned, faces like sunflowers
        tilting up towards
a welcoming Christ under whom devils
        carry out executions
like hair-spiked afterthoughts, and
        bells ring golden.

ALLEGORY OF IMMORTALITY

by Giulio Romano

Our world's dizzying clockwork:
horses, the mainsprings,
a phoenix who upturns a man
and pours him headlong
onto a god who vomits a waterjet.

An armillary jangles its celestial
rings above a sphinx who rattles
Necessity's chains. In a boat,
a woman-creature, taut
as an alarm hammer, glares

at a man-creature. He rows
tarred tides, quizzical, solicitous,
lecherous. I search for a place
to settle my eyes – there,
against a cloud, the Ouroboros

leans like a plate on a mantel
witnessing a generation's drama.
I'm overcome with a wave of nausea.
My siblings and I are the cohort
left standing. The canvas –

a gear tooth – punctures
my quotidian notion of immortality,
reminds me that the torque
behind my day is transience,
that I, too, only have so long.

DROP CURTAIN FOR THE BALLET *PARADE*

by Pablo Picasso

Mercury stands centre stage.
Dressed as Harlequin, he fixes on
a winged girl. She wears a tutu, stands
on Pegasus's back and strikes a one-
legged pose with an élan
that risks hurling her into the cosmos.

Picasso shed cubism for the design,
chose the music hall and vaudeville:
Pegasus encircling a foal,
a monkey on striped ladder, a clown.

Parade's premier flops: its cubist
sets enrage, Cocteau's script overreaches,
Erik Satie branded composer for typewriters
and rattles. Parisians fling oranges.
But Picasso's drop curtain enchants,
raises him beyond his station –

he meets elegant Olga,
a Russian ballerina. Marries her, moves
into chic lodgings in Paris where he presides
over the art world.
                          Finds his place at last.

A starry sphere lies at Pegasus's feet.

THE CITY RISES

by Umberto Boccioni

There are no shadows in this city
        just smokestacks and scaffolding
        spanning an angled vista.
Centre stage, a vermillion work-
        horse charges, its harness
        pointing upwards, as if it were winged.

Lower, a roil of faceless men in impossible
        elongated postures toss
        in an apocalyptic turmoil.
One man, arms flailing, lies prone
        in the path of hooves.

Boccioni holds the pen on the *Manifesto*
        of the Futurist Painters,
        espousing power, speed,
technology, violence, and war. (War
        would sweep away past failures
        and renew the world.)

Five years later, he is thrown from his steed
        during a cavalry training exercise.
        Trampled to death at thirty-three.
As if victim of his own doctrine.
        His brush foreshadowing his own demise.

TIME IS A RIVER WITHOUT BANKS

by Marc Chagall

A clock rides the river –
winged fish perched, set to dive
into the waterway
       like a stricken Hawker Hurricane,
body ablaze from the century's wars.

The fish's lipstick mouth –
how we distract ourselves from such
goings on – the clock's face
       blasé

       and time, being unstoppable
           as it rounds earth's grid
       (yet rarest of commodities)
inside its cheek, a gold pendulum
poised to strike on a whim.

THE TOWER OF BABEL

by Pieter Bruegel the Elder

A coastal city on a moody day.
Ocean-greens and sandy-creams
loosen shoulders. Between the waterway
and the town's edge, a tower rises
into the clouds. A closer look exposes
a farrago of frenzied activity:

ant-like engineers, masons
and labourers who haul and lift
stone in an apparent rush
against time. Bruegel renders a giant
treadmill, paints winches, cranes,
and hoists with technical exactitude.

Still something's not quite right.
Where the skyscraper nudges the city –
a sinking into the ground. No one seems
to notice. Within the interior, porticos
stand perpendicular to the lean. And oh –
the brick foundation is unfinished.

I want to believe in such allurements –
that those ramp workers keep busy
to avoid seeing the lean. Denial
a way to forgive myself for allowing
the entrapment. Too much mettle needed
to see failure, a blight on the shore.

MAGDALENE WITH TWO FLAMES

by Georges de La Tour

Mary Magdalene sits before a mirror
whose glass reveals the candle's hidden side.
Some days I understand the pathway.
Jewels are strewn next to her red brocade
hems. Propped on her lap, a skull.
Other days I am lost. Her eyes stare
into the darkness beyond. *I search
for the parable's missing word.*
She folds her hands over the skull.
An angled light falls on her face and neck,
forms a heron in flight. Something
is being revealed. *Then I find it.* Mary soars
above history's sentence – enters the quiet
inner perfection of the nautilus shell.

WITHOUT BEGINNING OR END

JOHN

Marie's chaplet feeds the woodstove's hunger. Angst grips
John's throat. With a staccato hand, he yanks it out.
A small mishap. The beige beads must have slipped into
the newspaper's folds. He stokes the fire with it in fury –
a rage that riles his guts. An Acadian incarnation of Zeus.
Does he want the beads to burn …? His right-hand fingers
pulse. Charred mouths riddle Marie's wooden rosary –
she will be upset. He never wants to ruin Marie's day.
But he does. All the time. His men call him John Bull.

Henri enters the summer kitchen. There, he cups Marie's
elbow, and ushers his mother away. Returning to the
wooden bench, he begins to churn butter. Had he seen
one of his sisters paddling the mixture, he would have
continued on his way. Marie, goddess of motherhood.
Marie, a Leto, landed in Acadia, linking with its
unmoored people. Marie, like the alfalfa butterfly flitting
over hayfields, pats Edward's shoulder, rubs Almira's
back, slips a sweater on Lorraine, all the while peeling
potatoes. Modest Marie, Marie without desires. Marie,
calm as the Northumberland's oily surface on a summer
afternoon. In photographs, she never smiles.

Morning rain spills over John's clover field. Marie reaches
into the kitchen-linen drawer and pulls out the calico
apron from under the folds. Its adjustable waistband
signals a gathering life in her belly. Alma wrinkles her
nose. Walks out of the kitchen. (She will walk away.
Barely sixteen. Remain childless.) Louisa steers the
children behind the summer kitchen to wash their hair
and sun-tanned bodies under the rainspout. (Louisa will
become a nun.) After Marie's twelfth childbirth, her last,
she bleeds and bleeds. Weakened, she remains in bed for
two months. Levigna, barren sister-in-law, enfolds the
newborn. Later, refuses to return Yvon. John wheedles
Marie – *Paul needs a son*. Like Leto, Marie hides behind
a veil. A button slips out of its buttonhole.

The narrow-leaved plantain slows its growth. Marie
hems. She is proud of her work: a mid-grey ulster tweed.
Belted in the back with adjustable buttonholes. Cuffs.
Notched lapels as wide as Cap-Pelé's winters. John will
overlap them to keep warm. Until she met him, she was
unattached to the ocean – his was the arm that carried
her full circle into this yellow farmhouse by the sea, with
its gables, porches, and green trim. During his fits of
rage, her small muscled architecture flutters around him,
zigzags upwards and sideways. Trying to fix. (He won't
harm her, nor the children.) Over the years, their threads
tighten into a continuous seam.

The train can't go fast enough. Towards her heart. When Marie was eight, her widowed mother left the children to earn money in Massachusetts. She has now sent out for her. Twelve years old. A new dress hangs in a new wardrobe. New slippers sit at the foot of the bed. In the years that follow, her mother teaches her how to apply twill tape to the roll line, baste hair canvas, pad-stitch. The art of hand-tailored buttonholes. As Marie presses seams open, the unsteady sway inside her steadies. Textured threads and weft yarns overlock distressed edges. At sixteen, she attends her mother's deathbed. A needle jabs her mid-thigh.

Black soot churns at the foot of a vertical drop. Besieges
Marie's chamber. Right arm shadowing her eyes, she slips
out of bed. Through the window: curtains of crow-black
ash. In the yard below, Marie's brothers swirl in a cinder
vortex. *Save yourselves*! she screams. A large hand rocks
her shoulder quietly. *Marie. Marie. You're dreaming*.
John, reaching into Marie's sea-coal darkness. The night
he spoke of marriage, he spread a sun-filled dawn at
her feet.

Snow swells over fields like a white wavy ocean. John wakes, flattened under winter's cloud. Fatigue anchoring his heels, he lumbers into the kitchen. Sky and weather god, he begins to hurl thunderbolts toward his family gathered at the breakfast table. *Children! House! Livestock! Clients! Bosses! Mortgage! Why him? There'll be no Christmas this year*. John likes his toast burnt, recalls Marie. At noon, he drives away in his Model T. Returns with bags of raisins, nutmeats, crystallized fruit. Oranges for the children's stockings. Marie's hand muffles her mouth. Quiet and swift, she separates raisins, measures nuts and chops fruit, all for tomorrow's pudding.

JOHN WILLIAM BECOMES
A BREADWINNER AT FOURTEEN

A wedge of sky drives itself into Cap Enragé's reef,
sheering off a jagged cliff. Fourteen. Father dead. John
becomes breadwinner for his siblings. At a lumber camp,
he moves with the relentless purpose of the Fundy tides.
He shoulders an axe, draws a crosscut saw. Ciphers how
many felled logs will fill lumber mill orders. John corrects
his foreman. Then becomes one. (Daniel, my father, stood
in line during the Great Depression, hoping for a job.
Talk abounded. *John William's lumber camp? Be warned.
He's hard on his men.*)

The crop is in. The Blue Bird crock brims with salted beans. Chow-chow relish, crab apple compote, and mincemeat gleam multihued on the summer kitchen shelves. When it's nap time for the younger children, Marie peruses Eaton's *Fall & Winter Catalogue*. A stolen hour. Pauses at the latest version of the Joan hat. Without beginning or end. She removes her own felt hat from the bandbox, snips off last year's adornments. Tucks in the crown and tacks it. Steams and reshapes the brim to find a jaunty tilt. Now for grosgrain and a feather. The hat perches at the end of her arm. She turns it admiringly. Gloom wiped clean from the oil lamp chimneys.

Days before John's return from camp, his children set to
their tasks: Hammer back in the tool shed! Buggy polished!
Front grass cut! Tiger lily beds weeded! An abandoned
rake might be a trigger for a choler that spoils the day.
Once home, John longs for the strange tranquility that
extends beyond centuries. He watches his household
unfold its symmetry. A sung "Ave Maria." Lorraine grips
his chair arm to stand. He picks her up, his youngest, his
last child. Rocks her. Later regrets, watching his son-in-law
clown with his children – not playing with his own.

Broadleaf plantain lines the drive to the farmhouse. When
Marie's firstborn son smiled, a smidge of light entered her.
As Albert grew, his triumphs shaped a sunrise. So dashing
at twenty in the suit she tailored for him. Mute, she rocks
in the chair by the kitchen window where she caught her
last sight of him: Albert, storming down the drive, hair
bristling. Another argument with his father. What was the
problem? Her Albert. Felled by a tree. A tree! The fabric
of her ripped from top to bottom. In her black dress,
black hosiery – she tells her dutiful daughter to dye the
kitchen curtains black. (Méline will ignore the request.)

Marie guides two visitors into the bedroom, opens a
drawer, and removes a silk nightgown. An embroidered
handkerchief. A box of Dutch chocolates. Gifts Alma
sent from Boston. Marie extends her arms and offers the
bounty to her guests. Each day, a gentle wave concludes
on shore. Each day, Marie pushes away the fibres of her
life. She has lost the joy of it. As in the carding of a sheep's
fleece, all this discarding allows the sky to show through
her. An indigo cloud scrapes its belly over the house's
gables. Overnight, like a ginkgo tree's synchronized leaf
drop, Marie's left side lets go. Her children refer to the
stroke as *mother's shock*.

Marie daubs John's burns with cool tea. Tannic acid
is good for burn – he read about it in *Maclean's*. The
Northumberland sets each wave on shore with fresh
intent. Like an aged tree, John's roots are exposed.
Receiving a letter from one of the children engenders the
same ritual. He pushes his rocking chair next to Marie's.
Shoulders forward, he leans into the words. Reads aloud.
His voice mounts into a crescendo – pauses – then breaks
into a high-pitched sob. Marie, quiet, wipes her mouth
with her hankie. Each letter rouses the same voice timber
in John – not unlike the sound of a bleating sheep.

You never called me by my name, wiped away
conversation with an embroidered hankie. Speckled hazel
eyes pooling placidly. Day chilled you, so my mother
crocheted a woollen shawl. Your fingers worried its
fringes. At the tip of Christmas morn, you appeared in a
green Donna Karan. Eyes – now glittering red goldstones.
With the no-nonsense confidence of Miranda Priestly in
The Devil Wears Prada, you pressed your mouth onto
my forehead. A heap of shoe boxes dislodged from my
closet's top shelf, toppled around us.

MY GRANDFATHER JOHN

As an old man, you rocked inside a sunlit rectangle.
I never jumped onto your lap. At bedtime, I'd watch you
eat doughnuts, drink cups of cream. Yet in a family photo,
you sit lean, large Picasso fingers curled around the chair's
arm. Your eight surviving children surround you, young
adults with actor-like good looks. Square pose steely. Eyes
like glass over river water whose depth betrays profound
fatigue. My mother spoke of your tantrums, how they
were the root of her intractable anxiety. Fear is a rope
that ties everything together.

"Between Thoughts": Charles Baudelaire, "Bénédiction,"
Les Fleurs du Mal, 25.

"On a Swath of Land Bordered by the Northumberland
Strait": Charles Baudelaire, "Sed Non Satiata," *Les Fleurs
du Mal*, 6.

"Vatican II Opens the Church's Window": Charles
Baudelaire, "Les plaintes d'un Icare," *Les Fleurs du Mal*, 12.

"Two Continents": Charles Baudelaire, "L'Ennemi,"
Les Fleurs du Mal.

"*There is no why*": Title: Philippe Petit's answer when
he was asked why he chose to walk on a cable between
the World Trade Center towers. Charles Baudelaire,
"Bénédiction," *Les Fleurs du Mal*.

"Philippe Petit as Prometheus": Charles Baudelaire,
"Bénédiction," *Les Fleurs du Mal*, 54.

"Posthumous Visit": Charles Baudelaire, "L'amour
du mensonge," *Les Fleurs du Mal*, C, 4.

"Divine Motion, 1992": Charles Baudelaire, "Le balcon,"
Les Fleurs du Mal, 28. Poem inspired by Philippe Petit's
walk to celebrate St John the Divine's centennial in New
York City, 1992.

"Why Père Chabert Wept When He Read Baudelaire to His First-Year University Class": Charles Baudelaire, "La Géante," *Les Fleurs de Mal*, XIX, 5.

"Père Chabert and the Passion": Charles Baudelaire, "L'homme et la mer," *Les Fleurs du Mal*, XIV, 10.

"A House in Chile, a School in l'Acadie": Charles Baudelaire, "Semper Eadem," *Les Fleurs du Mal*, XL, 2.

"In the Background": Charles Baudelaire, "Le Crépuscule du Matin," *Les Fleurs du Mal*, CIII, 20; Pablo Neruda, "The Infinite One"; John of the Cross, "The Dark Night."

"Père Chabert's Legacy": Charles Baudelaire, "Le Voyage," *Les Fleurs du Mal*, 45.

"You Will Walk along the River": Charles Baudelaire, "L'Homme et la mer," *Les Fleurs du Mal*, XIV, 1.

The title of "*And for a Father Hear a Child*" is taken from a line in "Hymn to the virgin" by Sir Walter Scott (words to Schubert's "Ave Maria").

ACKNOWLEDGMENTS

To my friends and family: thank you for your love and constant support.

Without Beginning or End would not have been possible without my editor, Jim Johnstone, who inspired and motivated me to complete my final poems.

I am grateful to the Ruby Tuesdays poets, who have been instrumental in my growth as a writer.

Thank you to Denis De Klerck at Mansfield Press for believing in my work and publishing my first book.

My great appreciation to McGill-Queen's University Press – it's an honour to be included in the Hugh MacLennan Poetry Series.

Professor Allan Hepburn, I was truly moved by your praise for this book.